The Burning of Los Angeles

THE
BURNING
LOS OF ANGELES

Poems
SAMUEL *by* MAIO

Library of Congress Cataloging-in-Publication Data

Maio, Samuel, 1955–
    The burning of Los Angeles : poems / by Samuel Maio.
        p.   cm.
    Includes index.
    ISBN 0-943549-45-0 (alk. paper). — ISBN 0-943549-44-2 (pbk.: alk. paper)
    I. Title
PS3563.A384B87   1997
811' .54—dc20   96-38810
                                                                                          CIP

Published by Thomas Jefferson University Press at Truman State University in Kirks-
ville, Missouri 63501 (http://www.truman.edu/tjup/).

The paper in this publication meets or exceeds the minimum requirements of the
American National Standard—Permanence of Paper for Printed Library Materials,
ANSI Z39.48 (1984).

CONTENTS

Part One
THE BURNING OF LOS ANGELES

The Burning of Los Angeles	2
Look	3
The Real Thing	4
Face Value	6
The Dispassionate Shepherd's First Blind Date	7
Regrets Only	8
The Handsome Poet	9

Part Two
DOMESTIC VIOLENCE

Love Song	12
Vague Scene	14
Projections	15
Peering in Her Lover's Bedroom Window	16
The Order of Insignificance	17
The Palm Reading	18
The Letters	19
Artist's Model	20
Domestic Violence	21
Midlife Epitaph	22
Reflections from a Pastel-Covered Box	23

Part Three
THE MINISTERS OF CULTURE

The Company Party	26
Had I Had Had Shakespeare as a Student	28
Inspired by Catullus	29
Art History Survey: Vermeer	30
The Paintings of Arnesti Gaspári	31
From the Notebooks of Count Galeazzo Ciano	32
Pilate	33
The Great Tradition	34

Part Four
"PEOPLE COME TO CALIFORNIA TO DIE"

Protestors at Disneyland   36
The Jack London Nuthouse   38
Whisky à Gogo   40
Club Casanova   42
Nude   44
The Filmmaker's Wife   46
Black Monday   47
The Spokesperson for His Generation   48
In Memoriam   49

Part Five
RETURNS

Southcentral L.A.   52
6th Avenue, L.A.   54
The Stranger   55
Winter Story   56
I Remember   57
Gathering *Funghi*   58
Late March, Trinidad, Colorado   59
Making Connections: Since the Close of the Allen Mine   60
Local Deaths   61
    I. The Dream   61
    II. Dream Life   62
    III. Glass House   65
    IV. Dark Woman Well   66
    V. Last Letter to John Milton   67
    VI. Pastoral before Dying   71
Father Death   72
    I. Telling Time   72
    II. Father Death   73
    III. At the Funeral Mass   74
    IV. Family Graveyard   76

Index of Titles and First Lines   79
About the Author   81

Acknowledgments

The author expresses his gratitude to the editors of the periodicals where many of the poems in this book were originally published (sometimes in slightly different form), as follows:

Antioch Review: "Vague Scene"

Bloomsbury Review: "The Stranger"

Chariton Review: "Look," "The Real Thing," "Face Value," "The Burning of Los Angeles," "Nude," "The Dispassionate Shepherd's First Blind Date," "The Handsome Poet," "The Filmmaker's Wife," "In Memoriam," "Glass House," "Club Casanova," "Whisky à Gogo," "Protestors at Disneyland," "Art History Survey: Vermeer," "From the Notebooks of Count Galeazzo Ciano," and "The Paintings of Arnesti Gaspári"

Cimarron Review: "Gathering *Funghi*"

Edge City Review: "Projections," and "Reflections from a Pastel-Covered Box"

The Formalist: "The Company Party," "Pilate," and "The Spokesperson for His Generation"

High Plains Literary Review: "I Remember"

Italian Americana: "The Dream," "Family Graveyard," and "At the Funeral Mass"

Mockingbird: "Inspired by Catullus"

New Mexico Humanities Review: "Southcentral L.A."

New York Quarterly: "Had I Had Had Shakespeare as a Student"

Northwest Review: "Dark Woman Well"

Paintbrush: "Regrets Only," and "Black Monday"

St. Andrews Review: "The Palm Reading"

San José Studies: "Love Song," "The Jack London Nuthouse," and "Reflections from a Pastel-Covered Box"

South Carolina Review: "Love Song," and "The Jack London Nuthouse"

South Dakota Review: "Peering in Her Lover's Bedroom Window," "The Order of Insignificance," "Domestic Violence," "Midlife Epitaph," "6th Avenue, L.A.," "Winter Story," "Dream Life," "Last Letter to John Milton," and "Making Connections: Since the Close of the Allen Mine"

The Southern California Anthology: "The Letters"

Sparrow: "Gathering *Funghi*"

Voices in Italian Americana: "Artist's Model," and "Father Death"

Whole Notes: "Pastoral before Dying"

"6th Avenue, L.A." also appears in *South Dakota Review: Poetry 1963–1991,* and "Midlife Epitaph" in *American Dream* (Youngstown, Ohio: Pig Iron Press, 1996)

[H]e could see all the rough charcoal strokes with which he had blocked it out on the big canvas.... Through the center... came the mob carrying baseball bats and torches. For the faces of its members, he was using the innumerable sketches he had made of the people who come to California to die; the cultists of all sorts, economic as well as religious, the wave, airplane, funeral and preview watchers—all those poor devils who can only be stirred by the promise of miracles and then only to violence.

Tod Hackett in Nathanael West's *The Day of the Locust*,
conceiving his painting, "The Burning of Los Angeles"

[H]e could see all the rough charcoal strokes with which he had blocked it out on the big canvas.... Through the center ... came the mob carrying baseball bats and torches. For the faces of its members, he was using the innumerable sketches he had made of the people who come to California to die; the cultists of all sorts, economic as well as religious, the wave, airplane, funeral and pre-view watchers—all those poor devils who can only be stirred by the promise of miracles and then only to violence.

Tod Hackett in Nathanael West's *The Day of the Locust*,
conceiving his painting, "The Burning of Los Angeles"

Part One

THE BURNING OF LOS ANGELES

[T]hey came here by train and by automobile to the land of sunshine, to die in the sun, with just enough money to live until the sun killed them.... [E]very morning you'll see the mighty sun, the eternal blue of the sky, and the streets will be full of sleek women you never will possess, and the hot semi-tropical nights will reek of romance you'll never have, but you'll still be in paradise...

John Fante, *Ask the Dust*

THE BURNING OF LOS ANGELES

The dwarf is the complete man:
WW II bombardier and Renaissance professor,
Club boxer and rare book collector.
He speeds the endless freeway in his Trans-Am,
Receives the praise of *scholae* for his estimate
Of the costumes and strumpets of the stage,
And is kept by his mistress, a fourth his age.
She's rich (parents in west side real estate)
And inviting: long legs and dark hair,
Her eyes feign innocence, her mouth a pout,
Perfect for entertaining—she's often sought
For dancing with more hula-hoops than anyone.
Just now she performs downtown, in Mexican bars.
Her agent/mother works to make her baby a star.
Her father she loathes for obliquitous attention.

But the dwarf sees only others seeing him,
Walking at leisure the Venice beach strip.
She totters above him on golden spike heels,
Resting her chin lovingly on his grey head.
He considers dedicating to her his next book,
Explication of child-porn texts *del Quattrocento*,
Written in Venezia, travel gratis a third NEH.
And after a life of studying Italian deceit
He knows nothing of cuckoldry? Friends she keeps
From his sight, especially the young comedian
Who mocks the little man with exact imitations.
Her svelte body undulates while she laughs
To the delight of this cruel Grimaldi, who bows
To her lace and bracelets, her fresh bikini wax,
The blue veins crisscrossing her right breast,
Her pale skin and black eyes, bulimic figure.

And the comic's wife waits each night at home—
The pathos of the most stock *commedie ridicolose*!
'Tis pity the dwarf spent his short youth other
Than reading Nathanael West, whose visionary
Foresaw the slow, smokeless burning of decay.

LOOK

The aspirant eyes of evening's promise
Center a columnar black and white ad
For Russian liqueur in *City's Angels*—
Flourishing dictate of sleek fashion—
While I, sole voyeur to know you drink
Only in positions of circumstance,
A feigned sipping—why, house raised
By sugar daddy boozed and steadying
For his nightly view of ornamental poses.

Each fine movement of customary grace
Freezes into another directed success
With those maneuvered by the study
And pleasure of your styling a glance
Commingling disapproval and longing,
Alluring acquiescence with lasting denial.

Like the overexposure of your gazing
Out the den window of your last lover,
The old and balding Batman five feet tall
And still bitter in his financial deceit.
Or the full page in this month's glossy,
The effected face, a viscous seduction.

Or as now, undressing for me alone,
Planned matching heart-shaped lace
And mannered elegance to your glide,
Whispering lined lashes, descending
Yellow lamp, intimate still life,
Without vision or voice, wax model
Self-sculptured and deftly rouged,
As for any audience, the projected
Look seeming to allow a possibility.

THE REAL THING

*"Neither of the pair immediately spoke—they only pro-
longed the preliminary gaze suggesting that each wished
to give the other a chance."*

Henry James

They were, too, the couple of perfect
Distinction and in particular taste.
Their confident manner when paired
In the excessive after-dinner scenes,
Or as the lingering night intimates
Of the illicit and suggestive allure.
And their knowing the precise image
To project, with slightest arrogance,
A complete emotion in exact timing—
Responses attaining demands of price.

That was their wish from the beginning,
Together in the vacant men's room
Before the full mirror, one evening
In early autumn, the warm and humid
Night ending with their making love
The first time, conscious even then,
Perhaps, of looking for the cameras
And their imminent expectations—
Of Mr. Black Velvet Suave's money,
And their certain self-defamation.

Working days, variations on theme:
A mirrored ceiling angled to reflect
The position of her face, a stained
Mouth parted in the accustomed "Oh,"
Silver glitter eyes like Cat Woman's
Confiding pleasure in seeing herself,
The slender thighs bathed in perfume
Contouring his neck, pressing closer.

Distinct from just themselves, each
Frequented movement should be real
By now, instead of vibrant exposure,
Their conditional blasphemy and hatred
For either life—possible or fantasy—
And for one another, the lost chances.

FACE VALUE

She sits before the lights of vanity
Completing her work with passionate ease,
Unmoved by my watching her make the face
To excuse her latest indulgent deceit—
"Forgive me?" the lowered eyes pout, allowing
For her many faults: hateful arrogance
Among others, too vulgar for poetry
To name—like her playing for the Greek dwarf's
Pornographos. ("It's art *and* it makes money!")

Yes, I forgive you. Routine making up,
Starting over, decorous dressing up...
And the value to me of her looking
As if she were mine alone for a night,
Without her indifference, or sacrifice,
Or her turning away those glossy lips,
Might endure beyond her fantastic fame—
As fleeting as her own flickering image
In a darkened little closet, in the mind
Of a lonely fan who doesn't know her name.

Am I better than this moaning lummox,
Drowning in abandonment, through half-shut eyes
Attentive to her projection of longing,
The suggestion that her desire is for him?
Each of us is the same—you and I, dear,
Locked together by illusion and lust
And rotting youth—the essence of your worth,
Pet, to speak for once with open honesty...

Something I'm not much prone to do these days
When I should be lying elsewhere—let's say
In my marriage bed, or to my wife's face,
Lies I've spoken for months anyway, since first
Meeting you one evening, sweetly scented
By the trimmed jacarandas, motionless
And intoxicating, like your still shots
Lodged in my memory, forever to stay.

THE DISPASSIONATE SHEPHERD'S FIRST BLIND DATE

Her clever and constant urging of him
To make a casual date, any evening
Or damning hour, restless, clouded, and blue,
As tonight, on Hollywood streets again,
Walking out his sadness among the girls,
The bulimic runaways, pale and scared.
Their scurrilous keepers hurry from sight
To alley offices when he approaches,
And the censuring priest (who might be real)
Stands by Frederick's, ringing for charity.

Where is the familiar, taunting chanteuse
Who seems vanished until his courage lasts?
Perhaps he's not to blame for her absence,
Perhaps his feeling nothing and alone
Deserves the loss of love and all desire.
She reminds him of someone else, of course,
The neighborhood's embodied substitute
For anything or one, now reflecting
His solicitude of guilt and remorse.

She appears!—and slithers for his dollars.
Everyone wants the money he doesn't...
She dons a black wig to please him for it.
Glossy red lipstick smears her reflex smile.
I knew you'd be back to date me, cutie.
To the palace, beds vibrating massage!

He sighs for the woman of recent past—
Never to return is too long to care.
Another tip, another smile...ten of,
His date allows answers to three questions,
Each the same, designed to resolve his doubt:
How long after did you remember me?
Once forgotten, how many long nights out?
And how many old men did you take in—
Queer Rossy, besides St. Paul and the dwarf?
Cutie, the response to all, *I'm yours true.*

REGRETS ONLY

Reluctant to accept his former friend's
Invitation to dinner, considering
The insulting memories he would foray
During the evening and long afterward—
But anxious, too, to hear about the woman
He once loved, years and lives and cities past—
He neither responded nor decided,
Attracted to the thought of her again
And an outcome more possible than before.

He would select more carefully the men
To whom he might introduce her—for one
Of the requisite age may buy her Florence,
As did the dwarf, or plead to her intellect
As did his gracious friend, now wishing to dine
And flatter himself, much using his tongue,
Dulling the time lamenting his losses.
Offering no hints of her history—
Her failures, he hoped—since leaving them both,
The evening would prove most unsatisfactory.

And she would desire yet an old man's comforts—
His money and leisure and few requests
For bedroom nights and idle gatherings
Showing her off to other flaccid men—
Should they chance to begin new, each wanting
Only pleasure still, without consequence
Or sacrifice of friendships and wills.

He would learn of her subtle deflections
Away from him, toward a more rewarding
Security than a young husband
Could provide in time. He would be left
With regrets only for certain decisions.

THE HANDSOME POET

You've an irresistible edge to you,
Something dangerous and something charming—
But most of all, you really like women
And that combination makes you handsome,
She says for once without that guarding wit
Her first and senior keeper trained her by:
"Create imbalance in the other's thoughts,"
It was his favorite lesson. "Always
Appear of interest, even if you aren't."
Less engaging, this attraction, with age—
Photographers no longer value her.

She appears vulnerable to the poet,
Her new sincerity flattering and warm.
He might compose a few lines about them,
Something graceful and something lyrical,
Serene and evanescent—though a lie.
He rather would prefer the portraiture
Of her that usually crosses his hand,
Images he creates from the last night
They were lovers, young and disdaining hope
For anything more beyond the moment,
Their motions of pleasureless performance:

"Yes, no pleasure at all while we endured
The end of it," the poem might begin,
"Those days of silence and nights of cruel
Taunting—until I quit, she was so strong—
And the prized face of her decade, so cold."
You've aged so well, he returned, *and retained*
Your good manners and bountiful wisdom.
"She loathed me then, but I thought it a game
Of her mother's doing, that paltry stick!"
You know, I've never gotten over you.
Go on, she tells him, *I'm most interested.*

Part Two

DOMESTIC VIOLENCE

LOVE SONG

We have lingered in the chambers of the sea
By sea-girls wreathed with seaweed red and brown
Till human voices wake us...

"Prufrock"

The new pier is concrete, the streets are paved.
The surfers wear short hair—nothing's been saved
Since you were last here, an epoch ago.
Everyone's faster and thinner than you,
The glassy bodies, ageless, browned, and bleached.

Most stands have changed, but the food still tastes of brine.
And the shore is constant, the day plays on without time.
The games remain, world-class and record-breaking:
A sleek-muscled young man digs and dives and spikes.
The crowd shrieks and shouts his name: "Troy! Troy!"

So once you thought you governed this beach...
Now, twice the age of girls catching you stare.
Surprised to find the sudden urge still there,
You glance away and study partial shells....
And imagine you'd still be received well.

You'd leave your life for the Filipina on skates,
Whose long black hair shines like copper in the sun.
It falls on her back to a perfect "v,"
Pointing to the cleft showing above her bikini.
She circles and smiles past you, smelling of lemons.

Down coast a Latina—or southern European—
Knows you're looking and shifts her hips in the sand.
She slowly smoothes lotion on her almond thighs,
Frowning in a glamorous pose she's gleaned
From the perfumed pages of her magazine.

You'll speak with that blonde, just now parting her legs
To better paint her toenails pink.
She unties her shoulder strings to tan—
What will you say? Your hair matches her zebraskin mat?
You hadn't seen her tall boyfriend playing catch.

Is your stroll over? Is it getting dark?
You've had this afternoon to your old self.
Late boats sail toward port, a family lights a fire and sings.
Your wife is waiting to nurse the baby.
They, too, mock your time and lead back home.

VAGUE SCENE

Francesco Vecellio, four centuries
In death, still without recognition
For his first domestic scenes
The *scholae* attribute to early work
Of his younger brother, Titian.

Unfortunate Francesco?
Who wants credit for initial failures,
To take responsibility for immaturity
Hanging before us in permanent frieze,
Or to remember obscure portraits
Of our young marriage?

* * *

At the small kitchen table
On the soiled linen, my supper:
Sliced apples, fettuccine with clams,
A full liter of *succo d'uva*.
Tonight I can desire nothing more,
Not even a job.

Sitting next to me, my dark wife
Longing to be pregnant again.
Her martyr's eyes glance upward, pleading.

Across from us, our four-year-old
Angel, golden curls and round face,
Searching his plate for something missing.
We imagine a luminous halo about him,
Brushed lightly in the wall's shadow.
His are eyes mourning the imminence
Of family loss, weeping.

PROJECTIONS

A sudden gift arrives from Mother, wrapped
"Boutique-Exact," the label says, with bows
And velvet paper, black. It's far from Christmas;
My birthday's passed. Yet Mother's sending clothes—
A way of mending us. We can't discuss
My life these days without my feeling trapped

In marriage or embarrassed that hubby's lame.
He doesn't work as hard around the house
As others do, she notices. But he's
Content to stay in place and won't carouse
(As others do) at every opportunity.
Besides, was Daddy any *crème de la crème?*

His frequent meetings often took all night.
He napped each afternoon. Our quiet play
Disturbed him anyway: the bedspread strewn,
His brow wet—restless signs his dreams betrayed.
He'd rouse upset, then leave as though immune
From duty. Mornings after, they would fight.

Twelve years, they never learned to reconcile.
We saw their breaking up before they did,
And found no answers in their gifts to us....

As now, another hint to have a child: a grid
Of silky strings and matching stockings, useless
Advice from one who wore too late this style.

Peering in Her Lover's Bedroom Window

"I see him lying in the shadowed dark
Aside his wife in her worn, pink nightgown.
Can this be his cross, the other woman
Who, I've been told, is loveless and barren?
She's calm, smoothing lotion on her pale skin,
And does not speak, for (he says) there's nothing
Left to say, not one more word about them,
About the deepened voids, the promises
Never fulfilled, the dying expectations
Of marriage and maturity, of believing
In each other enough to stay together.

"But watching her sit on the bed's cold edge,
Her back to him, veering as if in prayer,
Seeing how useless and alone she feels,
How she must have tried to make him love her—
As now, turning with a smile toward him,
Laying her creamed hands on his tensed chest,
Asking for his lies, for what he still finds
Attractive in her and whether he would
Marry her again, knowing all he does,
Neither deluded, as once, by romance
Nor encumbered by instinctual desire...

"And can this be my proud cock of the walk,
My Roman god I have soothed in my home,
Filling the brass bath of scented oils
With his muscles, curls, and assured presence?
I have raised this beast and left him wanting,
Breathless, my naked slide into the warmth
Of the water and my glide onto him.
I have seen him shudder and cry my name.
Can this motionless guile be the same man,
This sloth on his back as on a morgue's slab?
No, he's timid and does not even try.
This man isn't mine—I leave him to his wife."

THE ORDER OF INSIGNIFICANCE

I

The most banal of all things,
The recurring pain of lost love,
How you feel it at odd times:
Your second child's birthday,
A summer barbeque in the side yard
Of your large, new country home,
With few friends and patient wife,
The family life you can't leave—
Not the late hour, a cold night
Alone with your Jack Daniel's,
Thinking too much of yourself.

II

Professional hugs, wearing kashmir,
The first night sneaking away,
Faintly lifting your mouth no,
Knowing then the impossibility
Of more than your impulsive desire.
What made you again think of me?
Go to that rich old man—the dwarf
Who daily revels in the obscene—
You've long forgotten my love for you,
Our two afternoons a week, perhaps
An evening on the quilt in your bedroom.
How I hate you and your morals.

III

My party daughter favors her mother,
Strapped in high chair, slow to cry.
Making the salad, my wife stops
Listening to the conversation—
A job that doesn't entrap you,
The money to buy what you want,
Time to spend with loved ones,
The things that really matter.

THE PALM READING

The dark dream comes again
On the coldest night of the year:
You sit with your legs crossed,
Black hose and black heels
And your black hair spread about you.
We are in a strange room
At a table holding hands.
The full moon shines through the window.

Slowly, then, in a voice without passion,
You reveal the future of my life:
More clear nights, restless and cold,
More dreams of fortune,
Of a woman who left months ago,
And later, more women,
Each like the first—

Stop! I know this one.
A man, servile to his desire, thinks only
Of one woman, adulteress, continuous gangrene,
Pining for another chance alone with her
Maybe to slit her whore's svelte throat,
Yet hoping somehow to coo her love back.
His thoughts are of her always, even now
In the waking hour, the moon fading into dawn.

THE LETTERS

Few if five weeks after declaring
Your pedestrian complaints about love
And the exercising circumstances
Of this "or any such relationship,"
A coast line constraining apart
The fragile, crystalline surface—
The usual clichés, I was surprised.

More perfunctory "boredom and wills,"
"Egos, friendship," other pink songs
Concealing enough for me to hope,
To cushion finality with denial.
Some vapid compromise, and without
Your decrying our old charming look,
Wanting fresh touches or new flowers,
Maybe another assuaging long letter,
Maybe my words can pacify and soothe
From an endless, unmending distance away.

And then not, your indelible answer
As testament to my lack of decorum
And void presumption about language,
Its ability to change anything or one,
Arriving the last day—shredding fog,
The cold and the grey and alone—
Of someone's more serious life, an old man,
My unknown neighbor across the street
Who shot himself, the landlady said,
Upon receiving word from his daughter
Bemoaning the impossibility of caring,
Citing the children and little room,
Difficult finances, state home, etc.,
Her letter bleeding open, she said.

ARTIST'S MODEL

Seeing his pen and ink sketch of her
As the Sunday lingerie advertisement

the afternoon pallor of rain in Fiesole
the yellow light, the room's cold draft
and his not caring even to glance at me
I let fall the sheet from my shoulders
and offered to splay my legs for him
however uncomfortable in that off way
they all like and he always wanted
and I wantonly refused until then
I took his smudged hand along my thigh
but he was cross and would not answer

She remembered clearly his quick hands,
The black and thick hair covering them,
His alighting fingers brushing charcoal
Into mild grace of her becoming figure.

when he finished I was beautiful lines
and certain suggestion of empty shapes
my cheeks somewhat too high and sharp
and my brows arched and mouth downcast
little matters making me his substitute
for what he just lost and still desired
of another time and woman of that look
so he left undone my legs at the knees
an insignificant contour of the bodice
I parade in foddered background rising

Above all else, his dark, visionary eyes,
Seeming never to look where they focus
Or to see her beyond a scene's feature,
Necessary for its completion and life,
As the wind, rain, and light he creates.

DOMESTIC VIOLENCE

Another heat wave, though it is the season's fourth
Incessant month, more breathless September nights,
Open windows, tense, restless children lying outside
The sheets, and finally in the pre-dawn, a few hours
Of warm and mild breeze, a tenuous dream of leading
His wife up the stairs of a Motel 6 in the desert.
Her pale arms are tied behind her back, he is wedging
An L.A. cop's nightstick between them, pulling her hair
With his free hand, forcing her face down on the bed.

Waking in the pall of the sleeping pills (two, six?)
Following last night's habitual refusal, twice again
He tries and is denied, often, last week, last month,
Repulsed by the young mother of three, too exhausted
From a four-thirty feeding to arouse with pleasure.
They share the bed with baby's cries, old antipathy
And the stasis and frieze of their private history.
After the oak table a few days ago, the best piece
They owned, what was left for him to hit and break?

His certain memory of another woman, a surfeit time
In the early years of marriage and his first child,
Lacerates him most during such hours, and as he has
Frequently for a decade, he now studies his only two
Photographs of her, discreetly safe in Hall's *Chronicle*—
The Golden Age's heroic version of an idealized past—
A befitting tomb for the blurry and aging instamatics.
He remembers taking them, in front of her mother's house
The afternoon he drove her to a long promised audition

In Hollywood for the chance to appear in a variety show.
She's in black dancer's tights and adorning scanty skirt.
Practiced stare, her impatient poses mock his gawking.
He's melancholy and nostalgic…for this painted tart?
The romance never consummated, an affair they never had?
Here, at dawn, he sees with unerring clarity, how cruel
And foolish he's been, his unfair resentment, his wife
Turning on her side to feed their baby—affirming his life,
Shaming him into tearing the pictures, and becoming new.

MIDLIFE EPITAPH

"Remembering our once sustaining spouses, our youthful
And absolute promises to them, remembering the children,
How everything is a dividend of our supportive families,
How early covenants become financial burdens and gains,
Mortgages, profitable partnerships, cabins at the lake,
That church obligation, the school board, dinner affairs
Serve as auxiliary matters of delicate social acceptance,
That without a husband, a wife, all would be sacrificed
For ephemeral moments of imagined sanctuary from our true
Culpability, a willfully binding life we forged carelessly
In the exuberance of a beginning which propelled us here,
To a climacteric, the titillation of our princely toys—

"We make a facile decision to discontinue renewed hope,
Adolescent again, for the one consummate relationship
Fulfilling our needs, without resentment or constraint,
And capitulate to what we own instead of selfish desire.

"Do not grieve us before considering the eventual end:
The passion engendered by an arrogantly insular vision
Of ourselves soon would have betrayed us and vanished
Into the consequences of loss, our vindictive actions,
The orgiastic hatred of each other, of what we have done
And who we have become, miserly, self-deprecating death."

Reflections from a Pastel-Covered Box

Containing her life's most precious pictures,
All taken since their divorce some years ago.
How often she removed it from the shelf
of the bedroom closet and reminisced
During the final months of her dying,
Or whether she wished it found afterward,
Or how it came to remain the possession
Of a stranger, he didn't care to know.

He thought of her delicate hands wrapping
The box with a decorous precision—
Her deliberate measuring of his worth
He saw reflected in everything she left.
She would have let the lid fall gently closed.
Now it's opened before him, in the hands
Of his host for the evening, an old man
Filled with embittered memories of women—

Who explained anyway the strange collection
Of dead people's private remnants, acquired
From dealers in the macabre on both coasts.
"Unknown to me, every one of these dead,"
Said his host. "Not even as acquaintances.
I show their things for my guests' amusement."
The enchanting box was the first brought out.

"Let's guess, shall we, who was behind the camera."
"A husband," someone shouted! "Maybe not—
She's too happy," said a drunken other.
"A lover, then—look at this one in black lace!"
Asked by his host to offer the last guess,
He declined, turning instead to items
Other dead had left, hoping to find there
Something more personal to the living.

Part Three

THE MINISTERS OF CULTURE

THE COMPANY PARTY

A wife's astray. The professoriate-
Waifs muster at the liquor cabinet,
Imparting wagers on her dancing nude.
The chair invited every faction here:
There's chamber music, chatter, diatribes!
Who hears the poet ring the tinny chimes?

Alone, he enters, turns to leave...but then,
His name's pronounced in sidelong tones, so stays.
He knows who's speaking when he sees her group
Of toady students hesitate to smile:
The famous Marxist critic, wearing pearls!

She's denounced the poet's elitist tastes—
He shuns his age for Auden, Hardy, Yeats.
Using his verse as grist for her attacks,
She plans to cast his tenure marble black.

There's reason to celebrate! To cite blurbs
Indebted friends imagined for her tome
Enshrining avant-gardist poetry!
She collects poets like they're butterflies,
Refers to each by imprint and pet name,
And monitors their moves from school to school.

Preferring Gaudier-Brzeska to Vermeer,
Her bad teeth show, a canapé is loose
And falls much noticed to her ruffled blouse.
She eyes the Latina serving hors d'oeuvres,
"I fasted lunch today—to help the poor."

Uncertain whether they've been signed to praise
Her social action, show concern or go
Without the cheese and drink to blame the rich,
The silent students ponder what to say.
Their masters watch, and measure each remark.

Who's the philistine, who's the dilettante?
At the company party, everyone's
Examined and tried, the judges and judged.
Future decisions will be made tonight.
The Dean leaves early, the Chair begins to sweat,
The Chancellor's ill and calls in his regrets.

Had I Had Had Shakespeare as a Student

His freshperson year for "Composition,"
I would have closed both his plagiarist's eyes,
Averted his mind from those histories—
They're elitist, to be buried and done!
And as for Italian romance, cos, shun
It as sexist, vengeful, and cruel, those sighs
And all that plotting for some maiden's thighs.
Direct your spirit, I'd have said, to pen
Less comedy—for life's too serious
To treat lightly. And as for tragedy,
It's moribund, so male macho, and wrong!
I enlighten you, I in correctness
Free you of lies, slime, and patriarchy!
And never, ever, rhyme—that's for rap songs!

INSPIRED BY CATULLUS

To those who write out of others' spirit,
Edward Hopper's paintings (popular just now),
For instance, or Brueghel's and Bosch's and Goya's,
Nude Descending a Staircase and *The Starry Night*:

Either you long for professorial status to comment,
In your explicative wisdom, as one artist to another,
Or the most egocentric of you aspire to mythopoesis.
Or perhaps you are self-effaced, spiritually adenoidal,
And anaemic, so have nothing of yourself to give or say
Except the ideas of the Masters you think have inspired
Your creation—but it is nothing, too, like this verse,
Which tone and theme are taken from Gaius Valerius,
The laughable, caustic, lewd, bitter, naissant B. C.

Art History Survey: Vermeer

But not one word about the shades of light,
How the morning sun, even sieved through the opaque
And soiled windowpanes, circumscribes the room,

Casting luminous shadows on every fleck
In the aging white walls, every nailhole,
The peeling plaster, water stains beneath the sill,
The iridescent blues of the pictured tiles,

Raising each coarse grain of the golden bread,
Revealing the table linen's texture,
The woven designs of the handled wicker,
The weight of the rust clay pitcher in her hands.

She's calm and full, measuring the steady pour
Of milk, the breakfast meal ready to serve.
Everything is clear in nature's lustrous light,
Every essence defined by the coloring sun.

Why mention now *camera obscura*,
The nimbus shaping her young, yearning face,
Auroral waves alighting on her service,
When issues of today are so important?

Who wouldn't see "Maidservant Pouring Milk"
As domestic slavery is blinded
By the virtuosity of representation
The Dutch Masters bestowed upon the world.

THE PAINTINGS OF ARNESTI GASPÁRI

"It can't be done! The visage I wanted
On canvas, each detailed light in my mind,
And the misguided distortions I find
Drying before me—death, consecrated
Failing, mutations from *my* hand? Dreaded
Soul of no worth but this surreal slime!
Guido will pleasure to mock me in kind,
Filth-monger, his greedy eyes alerted
Only to gold, the scab, commercial worm.

"Yet he works daily, and his unworthy,
Stolen images sell. When will I learn?
My early dungeon pieces—let's carry
Them to Vesta's fiery mouth. So shall burn
The paintings of Arnesti Gaspári!"

From the Notebooks of Count Galeazzo Ciano

October 1942

The light wines he offered in the parlor
Of his Roman headquarters in the palace,
The Belgian chestnuts and brandied coffee,
All talk of politics finished for the night.
We moved at leisure about the large rooms,
Viewing the terrible art he commissioned—

Portraits of himself in furious pose,
Mostly, leading his high-stepping legions
Or standing erect before the red flag,
His stiff arm correct in peculiar salute.
This arrogant Austrian of common stock!

Imagine his speaking of the sublime!
How the Italians were too passionate
To make the Renaissance more than Beauty!
"Art must depict the world's direction, *Conte*,
Not merely show us its spirit and time."

How dare he address me in cultured tones,
Among shadows of his image, massive bronzed busts
Lining the front corridor, his warring brow
Dunning the few Masters allowed to remain.

No matter. They will outlast all tyrants
And countries, the Masters—even the Axis
Crushing beneath the blacking of his boot.

Indulge this monster for Italia's good?
Pompeii still displays the worthy governance
Of paintings and urns, statues and visages...
Enduring beyond the great triumvirate.

PILATE

O civil Rome! Let me command legions
Across new lands once more, conquer nations
And return home, marching triumphantly!
I've not the conscience for diplomacy.

My wife wakens, terrified by a dream.
I count the long days left to my regime
Among these fickle, nomadic people.
Young Jesus pledged to them life eternal—
They want him dead to prove he's not their god.

But who should decide? I? They, or Herod?
The issue is political desire—
Theirs and mine—not crime against the Empire.
Whether or not they are allowed to choose
To free Barabbas or this "king" of Jews,
Rome cannot yield responsibility.

Alone having the power to decree
The death of any man or miracle
And to render prophecies practical,
Rome fulfills all laws. Gods are made by us...
And we're to make another of Jesus;
Of victim, rule. Too late the countermands,
Of this matter I wash my knowing hands.

THE GREAT TRADITION

Silken flowing gown, golden symbol of *Pax*,
Sister-woven cope, in celebrious preparation
Of the Holy Eucharist, assisted by reverent
Boys, careful as ancient virgins tending
The sacred altar fire of Vesta's temple,
He, who begrudges fetid, political Rome,
Bishopric consulate decree, diocesan dicta—
Their assuming guise of obeying *vox populi*,
Foolishly to still St. Jerome's language
Of the blessed *Vulgata*, a celebrant's voice—
Arrives once more, the Great Traditionalist,
At his final chance to acquiesce completely,
Their largess of a celebret serving this end,
That of a parish in southwestern New Mexico
Of few, languishing faithful whose satin eyes
Emanate the mourning of their stagnant souls,
Their desirous importuning for God's words,
For the one, true, and apostolic convention,
So begins: *"In nomine Patris, et Filii, et..."*
To the quiet admonishment of the attendants,
Knowing the evanescence of even these words,
How quickly they will pass beyond our control
And then return to fall on one who deviates
From His most harmonic and righteous path.

Part Four

"People Come to California to Die"

PROTESTORS AT DISNEYLAND

"One Hundred Thousand Admission Today!"
One's somberly balked: His girlfriend protests.
Her thick legs are furry, her head's razor-shaved.
She raises a fist and screams she's suppressed...
But who can stir to care,
In line to buy clocks and ears?

Her chubby suitor has Easter-colored hair,
Lacquered to a point like the Matterhorn.
His fading black T-shirt is lettered despair:
Diatribes against the Windsor Queen
For poppy conspiracies
And the board game Monopoly.

Despotic Monarchy! Hierarchy!
It's the Capitalist Patriarchy—
Wrinkling when he folds his arms. Bloody drops
Tear from his press-on tattoo of a daggered heart.
He bumps toward frozen chocolate bananas.
She wants Styx-green syrup, a Daisy straw.

They're bound single file in a chained, labyrinthine path,
Her orange-feathered noserings dotting the loppy straw,
His light downy jowls jiggling sweetened banana—
Staggering a grandmother, foreign-shawled,
Just leaving the Haunted Mansion where she laughed.
The Pirates of the Caribbean at last!

A pirate's life and dress for me! Canon the rich! Take their
	jewels!
Course slowly by the moonlit restaurant, Blue Bayou.
Her cute pate glows mayhem in the cavernous dark...
Will she warm for Lobster Parisienne?
Dinner served on stepmummy's Am-Express—
The Beef Bourguignon makes his social conscience digress.

He'll yet impress her: Stop the Dumbo movie, Minnie!
Those jive jackdaws, loose-laughing, rapping crows—
Intonations of high-wired anathema.
Now Bambi indicts the hunting bourgeoisie,
The nuclear family—that's the snuff show
For Disney Dollars at Main Street Cinema!

Fantasyland's his best chance, Small World Cruise,
Sensitive lyrics—she squeezes his hand!
Would he offend to squeeze back? A sticky boy looms
For a character autograph, mistaking him—again.
She winks. Tonight, the Enchanted Tiki Room!
He pens: "Love, *Goofy*—from the Happiest Place on Earth!"

THE JACK LONDON NUTHOUSE

To Robert Lowell

A stranger looks across the bay at spires
Of leaden buildings rising through the fog.
He has stood dreaming here before, allured
By this view's promise of culture and grace
In the city on the peninsula.

If he could forget his experience,
He would envision once more—as he did
The first time driving over the long bridge—
A resplendent beauty awaiting him,
Instead of the world's open nuthouse:

A bedraggled prophet grasps the Bible
And shouts the truth to turning trolley cars;
A beaten poet spanks his hands for rhythm,
Recites a poem, and asks for money.
Even insanity is prosaic.

Two bald women dressed in combat fatigues
Hold a sign: "Every Man Believes He Is—!"
A tourist, wondering what this means, asks
For their flier. The larger woman tongues
Her friend's ear: "Don't give *him* one—he's a man."

A toothless man crashes his shopping cart:
"I am Jack London bridge falling down!"
Ionic façades break from the buildings,
Glass dances on the undulating earth,
A fire ignites along the sewage drains.

Concrete sidewalks and streets crack into smiles
And form a tributary relief map.
The trains' alarms panic; the gates are blocked.
The sane and insane are locked together,
Each running to find a private escape....

But the quake is distant now, the city normal.
The stranger wishes for another bay to cross,
Perhaps an eastern vista to survive.
It seems a little nudge would land him there,
That only memory could bring him back.

Whisky à Gogo

A smoky shout to the sweaty damsel,
A mouthed sham in return without a glance,
The dumbing bass ceaselessly au courant.
Mindlessly stirring drinks of Seinean water—
Caloric-phobic, nothing alcoholic—
They slouch on science fiction wall cushions
And feign to watch the bobbing dance darkling,
The only light swirling in rainbow crystal specks.
He's dressed in black, the ensemble's raiment.
Adieu, she pulls off her black sweater-dress,
Fluttering in ebony lingerie—no one looks.

Parisian as nearby Hollywood sets,
Whisky à Gogo, the rave discothèque!
Arrayal of costumes, leather and silk,
The leggings and tights, the jet miniskirts,
The vests and heels and slippers, some cottons,
Some linens, some corseted in black straps,
Black strings for brassières armored in gold studs,
Pointed and protective, sinister if small.

All cast by type, the danseur and danseuse,
The charlatan and escort, illusionist
And imports: *ciarlatore* and *cerretano*
(The mute chatterer and the blind hawker),
The predator upon the plunderer,
The purveyor and the pursued nymphets,
The croupier smiling with overtures
Promising new pleasures at more expense.

Muscle-bouncing Charon in sleeveless décolletage
Fords five dopey women across the gluey floor:
A famous chanteuse in jitterbug garb,
Her bedmate on ice skates, a boutade—
Yearning to ease her swollen anklets—
A maker of west side exotica,
A flinching bawd from Santa Monica,
And her pursed French lieutenant with crew-cut hair.

They sprint toward "The Black Room," Minos at the door
With his scythesque baton, assigning seats.
He collects and counts (It's *the* rave!) and offers
Now Lethe, Oblivion, now Ecstasy—
They choose and rise, like Phoenix, as someone else,
Aspirants again, ingénues, débutantes once more!
Floating on this *eau de mort,* evening into dawn,
Breaking over them last, downstream they go, go...

CLUB CASANOVA

"Watching her most maidenly
press her resplendent, olive-cream thighs
together as she, adorned in sable
designer miniskirt, lustrous scarlet spike heels
and matching silk blouse unbuttoned to her lace brassière—
a complementary pimpernel, I glimpsed—
all but knelt in the crowd, on the soiled carpet,
one jewelled hand politely on my hip for support,
I blossomed, completely without volition,
not several inches from her glossed lips.

"Yet even as she crouched before me,
pushing her Ray-Bans in place and dabbing
at the crotch of my chinos where she spilled
a double anisette flambeau, I did not think—
as I might have in coming years—
of calculating how best to pursue
to a carnal advantage this occasion
of being burned by a nubile.

"'Oh,' she rose, removing her sunglasses
to catch my averting eyes. 'That's sweet. Really.'
I remember now my misplaced twenties,
learning later that marooning evening.
She took me, to a dark corner booth
above the dance floor—an Arm and Hammer man
called Skippy quickly leaving when we approached.

"Sinking into the plastic-covered bench,
she slid close to me, draping one leg over mine,
running her hand along my inner thigh,
stopping short of the moan. 'Burn all better now?'
As I attempted to resolve whether
this to be the proper moment for our first kiss,
she slowly twiddled with my response,
once more spontaneous and beastly.

"'That is *so* sweet! You don't know what a compliment
that is to a girl—really,' shaking her head,
gliding her tongue over her whitened teeth.
I ventured a small kiss, her noting,
among her final words to me,
'Yummm, you've got the *soft*est lips.
You can date me *any*time.'
Then, standing to go primp, *sotto voce,*
'Say, what's your name anyway?'"

NUDE

Aging no matter what she tries,
Hating the lies
Of celebrity advertisers,
Their promises
To cover any natural flaw,
She now saw
Through them all: Her husband's chatter
That her
"Beauty" was "charming" as ever,
His clever
Deflections of the obvious.
Her present face
Is neither prized nor lamented.
She's tormented
By a lost portrait of self-worth
And fleeting youth.

Her secret dream in adolescence
Was no less
Ambitious than most of her friends'...

She pretends
Her bedroom mirror's a finished
Canvas
For which she's posed nude as Venus,
Who must
Be the subject of all great art
She thought.
Handsome men and important artists
Would attest
To her beauty and seduction
Always and again,
Her look a permanent pleasure
Forever,
Art glossing any imperfection—
But then,
Why be a model when you can
Just look like one?

She wanted to be popular
And sought after.
No one she knew visited the Masters,
Whose tastes were
Of another time and temper.

The Filmmaker's Wife

Daddy's metallic-yellow import jag,
Hand inlaid dash of cedar and brass,
Transcontinental telephone (for Paris
Chats, station checks, next location),
Soft Italian leather backseat wet bar
Stocked and fast, the dreamer's lair.

Waking late, another palish morning
In peignoir leisure, queen's robin eggs
Steamed and bitter, a sauna and oil,
The sulfurous mist of last night's run
Rising in waves like booze and snuff,
And vanishing as dissolute pleasures.

To displace her only permanent fear
With vapid and soporific indulgence
Might absolve the imbalance of horror
Measuring her life and desired wealth
On watching in seclusion the preview
Screening of his worsening fantasies.

She doubts this now, the high laughter
Panting as a robed man with a scythe
And a girl in webbed panties and bra
Chase to bed a frightened woman, her age,
The lustful nymph affixing a lariat
Around the T'ang vase on the bureau.

The woman submits with an odd alacrity
To the destruction of her possessions
Until she is satisfied none remains.
Then the crescendo of her screaming
Ends the film, shot here in this room,
Daddy still laughing beside her face.

BLACK MONDAY

A man stands alone, contemplates success,
Removes the Dick Tracy watch he promotes,
His diamond neck chain, silk socks, and shorts,
Then surrenders to waiting for his wife.

She's nothing if not his preferred reward,
Nothing if not the wife he most deserves
After the headaches, hypocrisy, the pain
In search of perfecting his salesmanship—

Which he has done to some financial gain,
But not enough to keep from being alone
This black evening, awake in bed, waiting
For the darkness in his room to lighten.

There have been other losses, other nights
With other women, more pleasing than kind,
And she won't be the last, but where is she?

The old man stared at him today in conference,
Gleaming a lurid dictum: "The right price—
Remember—and *anyone* can be had!"
Well, she was that night of early conquest.

Now it's his turn to lose all, isn't it?
A first in a career marked by many blessings,
For which he's not felt lucky or grateful,
But expecting them always forthcoming.

What made the old man turn against the watch,
This sure sell he guaranteed investors?
It's better than the comic strip model.
It's everything, it sings a lullaby.

THE SPOKESPERSON FOR HIS GENERATION

In the deep drawer of his unfinished work
Lay discolored scraps of unstudied thought
And brief sketches of fragmented wrought,
Images in sentences, his failed book,
The stalled beginnings, the hours they took,
Always too long, enduring days which brought
Him no closer to perfection or art—
Preserved for what, this monument, inert
Mass of unavailing craft, through at last?
There is no promise, no hope, no future.
In his night women, he's lost interest,
His wife's plans for a better marriage sour
And his children's faces fade to the past.
Even his own death note: undone, impure.

In Memoriam

"People come to California to die."

Nathanael West

On this coast where they once arrived destined
To fulfill the now distant promises
Which brought them here, each with a certainty
For success, these young, beautiful women
And thin, handsome men, few tired poets
And many vain prophets—all gathered to die
At last, among the glory and stardom
They created to crown and adore themselves.

Some came with talent enough to remain
Famous just longer than those before them.
Others played to fleeting audiences
Offering rhapsodic applause, when told,
Or unrestrained laughter when needed.
Everyone performed on this shore each night,
The sun benumbing their work by day.

We see them standing like the marble statues
Of the Renaissance they decidedly scorn,
Facing the sea, awaiting their time
To be called forth, impatient to receive
The final praise for their most current words,
Valued less than their attendant manicures.

We know what they will say when asked to speak:
In sands they've buried ancient art and thought,
And the world will end with them, as they've wanted,
Believing their fashion alone of worth.

Counting their gold, numbering their prizes,
They are silenced now and cannot endure.
They fade in the sun with their monuments.

Part Five

RETURNS

If not Los Angeles, then what? Where could I find welcome, where could I sit among people who loved me and cared for me and took pride in me?... There was a place, and there were people who loved me... I am going home, back to Colorado...

John Fante, *Dreams From Bunker Hill*

SOUTHCENTRAL L.A.

Leaving the University Park,
The daughters of movie stars,
Heirs of Disney, Goldwyn, and Getty,
The assured sons of money titans—
Each a loyal fraternity brother
And future privileged "alum"—
The insular boundaries of European
Brick columns and wrought iron,
The quiet Romanesque courtyard
Of the old philosophy library—
Its clock tower and gargoyles
Used in the original "Hunchback,"
Now hoarding in basement storage
A rare 16th Century collection—
Where today I nibbled cashews
And mingled at a special reception
Welcoming the selected summer
Honor students, gifted and aloof,
We're hoping to enroll next year
To gain on the private northeast.
Our lures are stately architecture,
The rose gardens and fountains,
Grand museums of natural history
And *beaux arts,* presently displaying
"Star Wars" tech-creatures aside
The Folger Shakespeare exhibit.
And frequent gatherings like these:
Good wines and dilettantes' talk,
A Dean's address, a pretty blonde
In a loose, off-white, silken gown
Delicately pulsing a golden harp...

Returning to the excluded nearby,
To the only duplex I can afford
In what we call "The Neighborhood,"
The Rolling 40s' owned territory,
I assume aristocratic detachment
And lower my gaze to their patrol
Of the long avenues lined by palm.

Poor men gather in the parking lot
Of the liquor store on the corner.
Its mad security cop once smashed
A drunk's crotch with a sawed bat,
Breaking the bottle of Colt Malt
Tucked inside his reeking pants,
While I watched from the counter.
And when caught staring was asked,
In a speech that might have been
The Bard's accentuated another way,
"What mixture you be, dear cuz?"
Alone in my Mediterranean color,
I am home, back to the mailman's
Delivering goods, Mr. Owl's Pharmacy
Dispensing crack, bennies, and ludes,
To the ice cream truck handling fix—
My neighbors get richer by the day.
And during the vast, sordid night
The circling police helicopters
Obscure the gunshots and screams.
The gang rapists and car thieves
Outrun them and sleep disquietly
As any of us behind barred windows
And steel doors hoping we're safe.

6TH AVENUE, L.A.

Tall palm trees sway slightly
In the warm Sunday breeze.
Children play basketball in the driveway next door,
The landlady picks cumquats for iced drinks,
Her husband slowly hacks the large banana leaves
That cover our frontroom window,
And we sit alone on the porch steps watching our son
Roll off the blanket onto the short lawn.
Shirtless young blacks pass, gliding to music
Of a radio they shuffle back and forth.
Here you never can be certain what season it is.

Deer hunting opens today back home, in Colorado.
I tell my wife the time my father took me up Trujillo Creek:
Our breath a mist in the air of beginning frost,
We wear red plaid jackets, track in silence,
Wade the cold stream, keeping alert for signs
In the stillness of mountain air.
He sights a six-point buck and afterward
Shows me how to dress it.
We drive into town, the blood-stained rope
Crisscrossed over the buck on the roof.
My father remembers the day Papa Saverio
Took him rabbit hunting in the hills
Surrounding Grimaldi, Calabria, and how he learned
To shoot the double-barreled *luparo*.
On Main Street a few lights are on.
Inside the warm car I listen to his soft voice
As I watch the sleet fill the dark night
With a winter we thought far away.

THE STRANGER

In my dream last night
I killed a man
Outside my house in black L.A.
Near my father's '55 Ford
I haven't seen in years.
The man called my name, drew near,
But I didn't recognize him,
The disfigured face of scarred flesh
Twisted above one, slit eye.
Unafraid, I stared him down
Then strangled him with my hands,
Laughing like Anastasia.

Awake before light
I thought about my boyhood in Colorado.
After school Guido and I walk in the snow
Over the hill to meet his father at the mine.
We stack empty oil barrels on the side
Of the old W. P. A. bathhouse and climb
Through the window to get warm.
Steam everywhere, water pipes
Hanging above us and along the walls.
A man, naked, hairy, yells to get
The hell out before we're hurt.
"Only one get hurt is you, old man,"
Guido laughs, "or might your daughter?"
The man comes at us, his fists wild.
We're fast through the showers,
The wet concrete floor.
He slips against burning pipe,
Grabs his face, "Jesus!"

Guido's father drives him to the doctor.
Turning to look at us in the back seat,
"Oughta kill yous."
I look away, feel his staring.
He presses the wet towel
To his red flesh, and stares.
This angry coal miner,
Crazy, sick for his daughter.

WINTER STORY

In the moonlight
I look across the field
of layered snow drifts
burying the weeds, the oak shrub
and yucca, the coral ants,
all that is dead for winter.
Behind the small dam
a piñon grove slopes
toward the frozen creek
where my father wanted
to take me camping.

It would be summer then,
the evening smelling of wet pine
and the fecund earth.
He would come home early,
find the dusty army surplus tent
in the garage and carry it
on his back to our site.
We would clear rocks away,
pitch the tent, make a fire,
eat pork and beans from a can,
and talk as we lay
on our sleeping bags,
drifting from the stars
to the clear blackness.

Many winter nights he came
to my room with his promise
of our hike, our swim in the pond,
the trout we might catch at dusk.
Sometimes he paused to look out
the window at my bedside,
tap kindly at the dark field
covered with snow, then continue
his good night story, just now
fulfilling its promise.

I Remember

The Palm Sunday in Aguilar
When I played the child
Who rode with Jesus (my cousin, Al)
Journeying to the Passover,
The burro sitting in the street,
The people, dressed from Mass,
Standing along Main all the way
To the hill near Pentasa's junkyard,
Waiting for their palm leaves,
And my balancing the bundle
Staying on pressing my knees to his haunches,
And Al pulling off the bridle,
Kicking that burro stinking sweat back
To old man Arnone, who led us,
Still in white sheets and sandals,
Behind the house to his cellar,
Lifting the rusted tin door
Down the fourteen steps underground
Damp, smelling of mold, dusty wooden barrels,
Lighting a candle, rolling a casque
To its spigot side, wiping jelly glasses clean
With his good hand—the other, a child's fist,
Truncated thumb, fingers lost in the mine—
Filling them with thick, *"Beve, beve,"*
Dark wine, braiding two strips of palm,
Using his mouth tying the yearly crucifix,
Rasping some story in low whispers,
Our knowing little of his Sicilian,
Imagining what he said
About Passion and Palm Sundays
In Vittriano, near the sea, the *baccalà* dinner
Keeping with the forty-day fast
Of meat before Easter—
The old man weeping, rising,
Holding the green leaf over the candle,
Watching it scorch, curl,
His rough hand marred even more clearly
Now in the light of the flame.

Gathering Funghi

Searching for mushrooms
I climb the Sangre de Cristo early in June
With an old man we call Magro.

The morning passes.
We separate at a clearing
In the aspen.

Near the bottom
Of a ravine I find the *funghi*
In damp shade.

I lift a flat rock
From the wild grass. The freed worms
Slip easily into the moist earth.

I pick the largest *funghi,*
Fill my shirt I use as a sack,
Then return to the old man

By late afternoon.
He shows me the way to taste
The stems for poison.

In the wine he's carried
We fry the good ones with garlic and onion.
Magro blesses our meal:

"Long may we keep the freedom of this day!"
He raises the wine jug. *"Salute, figlio mio."*
We eat by the plateful in the open air.

Late March, Trinidad, Colorado

    I am outside just after dawn.
    A light snow covers the field:
    The ant piles and the slag heap.

    A rancher lifts the lone
    Bale of hay off his pickup.
    A horse trots lazily to it.

    His slack belly drags close
    To the ground and shakes
    The snow from the dry weeds.

    It's old Chief Roman Nose
    Who threw me once in the gully
    When I was a boy!

MAKING CONNECTIONS: SINCE THE CLOSE OF THE ALLEN MINE

Cold stone house, dead winter.
Field dusted with light snow powder.
The father sits by gas fire logs,
Smokes, stares.

The impatient son leaves after lunch.
He walks across the field,
Down the sandstone embankment,
Crosses the river bed,

Dry now, as it will be even in spring,
Its course diverted
To accommodate the railroad
And dammed for the interstate.

He reaches the tipple,
Where his father and grandfather worked,
Now abandoned, rails disjointed,
Ties splintered.

The black, shiny slag heap
Rises above the clean snow.
But it is only ore, and there's no use
For the little coal left in this mountain.

The power plant runs
On electricity from the dam,
The railroad has no work,
Their coal cars fill with snow and wind.

He has nothing
To do all day.
Just like his father.
He is his father.

LOCAL DEATHS

I. THE DREAM

His dreams were hopeful of the future once.
Now, he dreams only about death, these last days,
And how he ended here, this far from destiny.

When a boy, he crossed the frozen eastern plains
Of Colorado alone with his father.
The ground blizzard worsened and the car died.
The grey dusk sky aged black as winter night.

They had not seen another car for hours
On the flat and barren two-lane highway,
Nor had they blankets, flashlight, anything to eat.
His father prayed aloud for a miracle,
Then, holding his small son, began to cry.

The car warmed, the blue light of a truck flashed,
A man knocked on the driver's side window,
Offering help. Soon the engine started.
His father closed the hood, turned to thank the man—
But he was gone, juice and cheese left behind.

The boy fell asleep, as they drove onward,
And dreamed his mother was alive.
She listened to his telling what happened
When they got home, and poured hot chocolate,
Kept the fire glowing, made his bed.
She tucked him in, saying it was an angel
Who helped them, that good things must be destined.

He woke, just then, blinking at the windshield
And filling with the certainty of promise,
A fresh dawn igniting the snow-covered day.

II. Dream Life

Of two lives I contrived
Unconsciously in my youth,
Attempting to reconcile finally
Desirous memory with a temporal
Vision of the objective world,
I choose the imaginary,
Elusive truth and constancy.

For this static instant,
An afternoon beneath the trellis
Of the old back porch
Of the old mountain house
In which I was born,
Having passed a life of illusion
In preservation of self-worth,
This moment in the faintest shadows
Of the fading latticework
Forces a choice, and I choose
To retain yet the amaranthine
Conception of being and time—
For the other, the disillusory,
Is the veracity of the nihilism
Of our deserved millennium:

Nothing, nothing waits, immutable,
Intolerable of change and rot,
Not the coal veins nor the dried
Grapevines dying above me,
Aged plexus of arthritic ambience,
Not one blessed or cursed tree
Or stone or fence remains
As I left it a lifetime ago.

The open range and long meadow
Yield to bankrupt strip mines,
Corporate desecration of prized
Mineral rights presently of no value.

Not the slag heap, overgrown
With the heavy seasonal weeds,
Down which we hiked in the summer,
Crossing under the railroad
Through the trestle returning
From walking father to his work
On the tipple, in heat or cold.
Not the great deep mine, emptied,
Seeping methane, employing no one—
How it was then is my choice,
In disregard of all perception,
Jackrabbit tracks in light snow,
Wandering without direction
After school and on Saturdays,
Our bonds of home and family.

Or the certain reflection,
Remorse, and small lives in fear
And anxious insecurity of a job,
Of remembering the people unable
To wait for me to decide, and those
I sent away by immature decisions.
Nothing, nothing, not the life
I have tried embracing again,
After cities and continents,
Death and anger, assuming time
Could wait for me to want it.
Not the girl from China Lake,
Her warm mouth and slender hands,
Nor her child, never to know
A teen-aged father who ran out
Of marriage, abandoning what
Might have been a pleasant life
In a coal town of closed mines.

Of two lives obscured until now
In simultaneous existence,
This, the truth I hide in choosing
The imagination of an innocent time.

III. GLASS HOUSE

The glass of fashion and the mould of form,
The fabulous mansion of Lemuel Ledham Fawn, III,
Who lived what his daddy (and granddaddy before)
Could only desire, only sadly bequeath,
This affectatious dream of ill-begotten culture,
Decades old, finally realized by Fawn too late,
Two generations later and far from the Acadian,
In Colorado, behind last season's alfalfa field
Beyond the black walnut grove, the empty house,
Splintered Corinthian columns bracing stubbornly
The swaying wooden porch where Fawn would sip
His evening coffee and admire the alpenglow
Of the surrounding aspen of Simpson's Rest
And praise the large marble font in the center
Of the front garden: a devil's wide mouth
Screaming three lines of water on one side,
Curly haired, round baby with wings on the other—
Now dry, nearly hidden in the spleenwort, forage
The unpaid gardener has not trimmed since he left
Half a century ago, the day Fawn slit his own throat
With the artist's sharpened carving knife
Taken from the cigar box that kept the log
Of not only the one thousand hours of work
He was cheated of, but the blackened reasons for it:
The family's history of deceit, their murderous
Quest for fortune and respect, the artist's proof
And the County Clerk and Recorder's receipt and time
Registering his statement just before returning
To the mansion he built to gather his stone chisel,
The imprint implement, and few papers safe in the box,
Hoping to earn enough elsewhere for a passage back
To his home in a southwest province of France.

IV. Dark Woman Well

Under the dark bath, the ugly death.
Descend to death, the rope to water,
The breathless boy lowered and cold.
His the fright, to lift the corpse,
Its yellowed face and bloated lips,
The old stone ground swell, opened.

Then set lower the boy and slaken
Another rope, knotted and readying
To surface in the shadowed summer,
As night buoy floating with ease,
The weighing corpulence, the sway
And slow rising through the center,
The cylindrical scope and closure,
The wet reflective casing, skyward.

Now spinning, his eyes closed to her,
An opalescence of sight and madness,
In reverie her barefooted fleeing
From trailer shack and bean garden,
From children next door she treated
To peanuts, and him to cinnamon bears,
Feeling not thousand thorns or gravel
The short way to the abandoned lot.

Bound in her density, pulled as one
·Through the circle opening to stars,
To the backyard of nursery rhymes,
The bricked paths and tulip rows,
Small white veranda, glass chimes,
All lilac memory, these tall weeds
And this rot where once the servant,
Returned in shadows diving for life.

V. Last Letter to John Milton

In Memoriam (b. 5/24/24; d. 1/28/95)

Friend Sam—Winter is harder on me this year than it
has ever been. Not sure why, except maybe age. But,
this summer (last summer) I felt good in California
and Nevada.... [O]n to summer & the West again, I
trust, and a good talk with you.   Warmly, John

last letter from J. M., 1/23/95

The consoling heat you've waited for
has finally arrived, friend John.
(What would a letter from me be
without a weather report?)
With an irony you're sure to love,
the first calendar day of summer
brought 105 degrees, in the shade—
a record-breaker, hot enough
for old coyote even, yes?
Two days before, it was a cool 72.
Only a lifelong Westerner can appreciate
the wondrous horror of such sudden changes
in temperature (extreme as it gets here),
probably because he's spent a lifetime
making, then renegotiating, travel plans
while trying to outguess nature.
For now, the days have settled
into comfortable 80s, foggy mornings...

So summer is here, and so we await you.
Everyone awaits you! Every place
you always stop along the way—
your favorite town, Winnemucca, Nevada,
that McDonald's pit stop
most people can't wait to leave behind
on their way to or from
sordid (but "cultured") San Francisco.
Awaiting are Winnemucca's dry heat waves,
rising, like sunstroked spirits,

from the blacktop parking lots,
the surrounding desolate desert plains
of parched sagebrush, piñon, and yucca,
the graveyard you alone of all visitors
can read like a history you might write
of nomads, natives, settlers at rest.

Winnemucca awaits you this year,
your one week stay coming to California
and your one week going back home,
your camera and nostalgic eye,
your soft heart and romantic inventions
of every peeling building and cathouse
and two-bit casino—you can see through
to their resplendence, their stories.
The Thunderbird has your usual room reserved,
the one you and Lynn have stayed in
the last hundred years straight.
Shall I write you there to arrange
our day for lunch when you get here?
Or will you (like last year) write me
from Santa Barbara, or call (like year before)
from the Golden Bear Inn in Berkeley?

For Berkeley, too, awaits you—
even if you hardly leave your writing room
(on the second floor, reserved of course)
or venture farther than the hotel restaurant,
The Golden Bear Café, with its Western flavor
and strictly fried food menu
and aging Western tables—like none other
in hip Berkeley or all the Bay Area.
How did you manage to find the only place
in this noisy, soiled, street-life city
that most resembles your beloved
Prairie Café in Vermillion?
Your favorite waitress awaits you,
the one you so admire for making it
on her own with no husband, no education
and two children to raise next to People's Park,

the one you overtip twice each day
in part for refilling your coffee cup
twenty times per sitting (hot, black, no sugar).

Remember our four-hour lunch there?
Everyone knew you, the regular customers,
the cashier, the kid mopping the floor—
everyone again greeted you,
many hadn't seen you since breakfast.
You introduced me as a "Western writer"—
and I know I haven't thanked you enough—
and we sat at your round table
in the corner by the windows
and got down to our usual business:
poetry, your first love and how
we most fully connect.

Auden came first, not so odd for us
but confusing to those who would typecast you
as having "regional" interests only,
then the California of Robinson Jeffers,
effete Bay Area academic, passionless poets
(you didn't know many), the self-promoting Beats
now college profs in tweed, still hating Nixon,
the self-serving, dramatizing confessional poets—
How many poems did you say you got
at *South Dakota Review* last month alone
beginning with "I," ending and throughout "I"?
And effete Plains academic poets (you knew most),
those fake Westerners who yearn for Boston,
who couldn't find work in the East.

Then on to your writing projects and mine,
books we've written, those we planned to write.
You qualified mentioning my poems becoming
"urbane" over the last decade as "a compliment"
and mildly cautioned against my obsessions
with meters, conventions, and rhymes.
(Well, how do you like this one,
maèstro, much looser, more reflective—

you've no idea how hard it's been
to make it so, the lessons
of the Masters finally sinking in?)

And stories of Fred and Max and Frank,
friends dead or nearly dead now, each put in
his time seeking your guidance
and critical judgment on manuscripts,
your honest approval—which never came easy.
And the Stegner anecdote, Wally
talking you into writing the history
of South Dakota when you would rather write poems:
"Hell, John," he said, "you have to write it—
you *invented* South Dakota!"

And so you did—you invented South Dakota
wherever you went, finding South Dakota
in Winnemucca and Berkeley and Monterey—
Steinbeck country you brought to South Dakota.
You invented South Dakota with the Milton signet:
clear, unadorned, heartfelt prose, in homage
to the people and spirit of your adopted state.
You invented the literary West, too.
Everywhere you went was South Dakota.
Everywhere you've gone is South Dakota.

Even summer in California, awaiting you.
We all await you, friend John, for we miss you,
for we need to thank you, to learn from you still,
to be in your wise, generous presence.
But for now, it's *ciao* in *la bella lingua,*
the language you love to hear:
Maèstro, sei il miglior fabbro.
Tanti auguri! Con affetto, sèmpre—

VI. Pastoral before Dying

The old Navaho has worked cattle since daybreak.
At dusk he leaves the dry plateau
For supper and sleep.

He dreams of wandering
Beyond the black walnut tree
Into the autumn light of a full moon

Across the barbed wire into the field of long grass
Where Montiero's herd huddles by the pond.
He wakes to their dank smell, ancient sweat on his face.

Outside, wind and dust.
Vague clouds circle the dark sky.
Dawn is near.

FATHER DEATH

In memoria di padre mio,
Ernest "Chino" Maio (1917–1986)

I. TELLING TIME

   after all night rain
three feet dawn haze fading
   into morning light on pasture
two weeks green with spring grass

   old man by steam radiator
wrapped with old shawl too small
   legs ache hours in rocker
effort just to rise and walk to window

   slow black angus in afternoon sun
one we pulled from Cragun's gully
   stuck in mud last April March?
she must have died years ago

II. Father Death

We die as we dream:
Alone.

And so I was alone
With my father
The morning he died
In the hospital room.
It was just after dawn,
A crescendo of light.
The patient
From the other bed
Was in the bathroom
With the nurse.
The running water
Woke me.

For days my father
Had not talked
Or recognized anyone.
But now he raised
His head slightly
Off the pillow
And looked at me.
I sat on the edge
Of his bed,
Leaned towards him.

He said something
In Italian
I didn't understand.
He spoke out of one side
Of his mouth
Slurring his words
Like he used to when
Making fun of somebody
He knew from Morley.
"Sollevami! Ascendente! Ascendente!"

Then he smiled, in peace.

III. AT THE FUNERAL MASS

The eldest son came from L.A.
To speak a short narrative
Of his earliest memory, age four:
His father holding him
Over the large drain sink
By the washing machine,
Rinsing his mouth for an hour
Because he'd begun to eat
Out of an open can of lye
His father brought home
From the mine and hid
In the garage.

The mourners—he knew each
As long as he could remember—
Laughed uneasily.
The son was so much
Like the deceased!
His father was noble,
The strongest man he knew,
The most ethical.
And *Zio* Orlando, his father's
Older brother and boyhood idol,
Told him later that day
While still in their suits
Playing touch football:
"Your father could read people
Just like that," snapping
His fingers. "Size them up
Just looking at them."
Then he knew:

Leaving the pulpit,
He noticed a beautiful, dark woman
About his own age
Wearing a black sweaterdress,
Black lace hose and heels
And a black velvet choker
Around her elegant neck.

He took his place
Beside his sobbing mother.
The Priest, before preparing
The Holy Eucharist, said:
"Praise be to God for showing
The father how to teach the son.
The father was first a good
And faithful husband."

The young woman began weeping,
Dabbing her eyes so not
To smear her cosmetics.

IV. Family Graveyard

Each time I visit here to ease
among the dead of Holy Trinity,
autumn leaves tremble softly
and fall on shadows of monuments
engraved with familiar names
and a foreign language:

Bartolino, Mantelli, Gaetano Amadeo,
Aggalina Arnone, Barratono, Mattorano...
Nato in 1880, '89, '91 a Grimaldi, Molito,
Reggio di Calabria, a Palermo, Siracusa,
Messina, now dead, buried in autumn,
Morto nel 1915, '37, '67 a Trinidad, Colorado.

Here lies Gianni Chaccione
"A Man Who Loved His Mother"
and artist with his Colt Special,
once shot himself in the leg as a cover
for killing a government mine inspector,
resting next to his *paisan:*

a bricklayer, lover of Dante,
who crafted the family stone
from a fourteen-hundred raw slab
of Sicilian marble, shipped from Amato
by his first cousin, Rosario.
Hand-rubbed with cardinal dye, polished,

an angel tilts a vase
of roses, each thin petal
miraculously detailed, stone spring
buds not yet in complete bloom,
encircling our name carved
in large, Romanesque lettering,

now marking where he too rests,
my father, Arnesti Giacomo, born 1917
in Morley, a few miles from this memorial
to his father. What more can I do?
"Questi ch'io ti cerno col dito fu miglior fabbro."
"The one I point to was the better blacksmith."

INDEX OF TITLES AND FIRST LINES

First lines are set in roman type, poem titles in SMALL CAPS, and titles of longer poems in *italics*.

6TH AVENUE, L.A., 54

A man stands alone, contemplates success, 47
A smoky shout to the sweaty damsel, 40
A stranger looks across the bay at spires, 38
A sudden gift arrives from Mother, wrapped, 15
A wife's astray. The professoriate-, 26
after all night rain, 72
Aging no matter what she tries, 44
Another heat wave, though it is the season's fourth, 21
ART HISTORY SURVEY: VERMEER, 30
ARTIST'S MODEL, 20
AT THE FUNERAL MASS, 74

BLACK MONDAY, 47
BURNING OF LOS ANGELES, THE, 2
But not one word about the shades of light, 30

CLUB CASANOVA, 42
Cold stone house, dead winter, 60
COMPANY PARTY, THE, 26
Containing her life's most precious pictures, 23

Daddy's metallic-yellow import jag, 46
DARK WOMAN WELL, 66
DISPASSIONATE SHEPHERD'S FIRST BLIND DATE, THE, 7
DOMESTIC VIOLENCE, 21
DREAM LIFE, 62
DREAM, THE, 61

Each time I visit here to ease, 76

FACE VALUE, 6
FAMILY GRAVEYARD, 76
Father Death, 72
FATHER DEATH, 73
Few if five weeks after declaring, 19
FILMMAKER'S WIFE, THE, 46
Francesco Vecellio, four centuries, 14
FROM THE NOTEBOOKS OF COUNT GALEAZZO CIANO, 32

GATHERING *FUNGHI*, 58
GLASS HOUSE, 65
GREAT TRADITION, THE, 34

HAD I HAD HAD SHAKESPEARE AS A STUDENT, 28
HANDSOME POET, THE, 9
Her clever and constant urging of him, 7
His dreams were hopeful of the future once, 61
His freshperson year for "Composition," 28

I am outside just after dawn, 59
I REMEMBER, 57
"I see him lying in the shadowed dark, 16
IN MEMORIAM, 49
In my dream last night, 55
In the deep drawer of his unfinished work, 48
In the moonlight, 56
INSPIRED BY CATULLUS, 29
"It can't be done! The visage I wanted, 31

JACK LONDON NUTHOUSE, THE, 38

Last Letter to John Milton, 67
Late March, Trinidad, Colorado, 59
Leaving the University Park, 52
Letters, The, 19
Local Deaths, 61
Look, 3
Love Song, 12

Making Connections: Since the
    Close of the Allen Mine, 60
Midlife Epitaph, 22

Nude, 44

O civil Rome! Let me command
    legions, 33
Of two lives I contrived, 62
On this coast where they once arrived
    destined, 49
"One Hundred Thousand Admission
    Today!" 36
Order of Insignificance, The, 17

Paintings of Arnesti Gaspári, The, 31
Palm Reading, The, 18
Pastoral before Dying, 71
Peering in Her Lover's Bedroom
    Window, 16
Pilate, 33
Projections, 15
Protestors at Disneyland, 36

Real Thing, The, 4
Reflections from a Pastel-Covered
    Box, 23
Regrets Only, 8
Reluctant to accept his former friend's,
    8
"Remembering our once sustaining
    spouses, our youthful, 22

6th Avenue, L.A., 54
Searching for mushrooms, 58

Seeing his pen and ink sketch of her, 20
She sits before the lights of vanity, 6
Silken flowing gown, golden symbol of
    Pax, 34
Southcentral L.A., 52
Spokesperson for His Generation,
    The, 48
Stranger, The, 55

Tall palm trees sway slightly, 54
Telling Time, 72
The aspirant eyes of evening's promise,
    3
The consoling heat you've waited for,
    67
The dark dream comes again, 18
The dwarf is the complete man, 2
The eldest son came from L.A., 74
The glass of fashion and the mould of form,
    65
The light wines he offered in the
    parlor, 32
The most banal of all things, 17
The new pier is concrete, the streets are
    paved, 12
The old Navaho has worked cattle since
    daybreak, 71
The Palm Sunday in Aguilar, 57
They were, too, the couple of perfect, 4
To those who write out of others'
    spirit, 29

Under the dark bath, the ugly death, 66

Vague Scene, 14

"Watching her most maidenly, 42
We die as we dream, 73
Whisky à Gogo, 40
Winter Story, 56

You've an irresistible edge to you, 9

ABOUT THE BOOK

Design and typography by Tim Rolands

Set in ITC Legacy Serif,
designed by Ronald Arnholm
and released in 1992.

One hundred copies
of this book were clothbound
and signed by the author.
This is number 74 *.*

ADP-0368   11/10/98

PS
3563
A384
B87
1997